The E.N.D.

(The Evolution of Noel Dior)

Noel Dior Gantt

All rights reserved. No part of this book may be reproduced in any form by an electronic or mechanical means, including information storage and retrieval systems, without permission in writing from the publisher, except by a reviewer who may quote brief passages in a review.
For use in academic or recreational settings please contact author via email at noel.gantt@live.com

ISBN 978-0-6920-7270-7 (paperback)
Copyright © 2018 by Noel Dior Gantt

Dedications

This collection of poems is dedicated to my strong, persevering, awesome, loving, and extremely 'bout her business mother of mine, Cheryl L. Gantt. She has been with me through my crazy ride called life at every speed bump, twist, turn, and even U-turn. I could have never made it this far without her but looking at her strength I sure would have tried. My mother is beautiful, bold, fierce, and the greatest Grandmother my daughter Nia could ever ask for. I love her with all my heart, and I am proud to be born of someone so fabulous, caring, outspoken, and always there for her family. I love you Mommie, I did this for you & Joan!

Also dedicated to my father, Iben Gantt, who has shown me time and time again that no matter how complex love and family dynamics may be forgiveness can remedy even the most daunting situations. During my evolution my father has proved that growth is a lifelong process and that every day is another chance to uncover more about life and realize truths about the world and ourselves. My father has the biggest heart that I've ever seen a man possess. He has the strength to speak his truth with vulnerability and no apologies. Being able to cultivate our bond has allowed me the opportunity to see exactly why I love the way I do, why I love to learn every day, and why I am on a never ending quest to expansion and self-liberation. Dad I'll always cherish you & your willingness to understand things from my point of view and your readiness to see the bigger picture. You are one-of-a kind! I love you!

Poetic Pain

Poems that weren't even conceived and seen on pages left photographic images in my mind. Their words echoed in my heart reminding me of who I am and how important it is for me not to let go. I've spent my life-giving insignificant beings' power and I surrendered rights to my mind, my body, and most importantly my spirit. I've beaten myself up repeatedly for not being who the world wanted me to be. Ridiculed myself for not believing what the world wanted me to believe. I've committed several cases of domestic abuse and I am on the run; I cannot be caught because the victim is me. A murderer I am, I drove myself crazy and lost my mind several times and beat myself up to the point that I died. This relationship I have with me I am sure it's unhealthy. I know no other way to live, I know no other way to be. I am the victim and I am my victor…only I can truly save me.

Awareness

Fire & Desire.
Mind is awake, body is tired.
You became less of a liar the more you got higher
Weakened shields.
Slow to yield & quick to build.
Put your mind to the test as your soul heals.
Be swift but cool.
Utilize proper tools.
Steer clear of fools.
Avoid getting killed.
Avoid getting bamboozled by fake disguised as real.
Trust what you feel, have faith in what you know.
Calculate your growth.
Multiply the hope.
Divide up all the dope and unravel all the ropes.
Reach your Nirvana and neglect to gloat.
Cope with reality.
Have hope for those hexed by the hoax.

Something More

There has to be something more for me
Something more beyond these grimy streets
Something more in between my nervous heart beats
that pound and pound against my chest like heavy anvils
that are equivalent to the thoughts that are constantly
weighing on my brain
And I don't know if any of you knows what it feels like to
be a prisoner of your thoughts but
it's tiring and I just want to break free
And if you are not completely grasping what I mean
I will try to paint a picture the best way my restrained
brain can
Imagine me
Body intact but on the inside my mind is racing back and
back forth and forth
Making all decisions for me
Letting my heart lay dormant and be a doormat
And it's obvious that my condition is detrimental
why did I have to be born with this over analytical state
of mental
and I haven't met one single person like me so I remain
lonely
And I probably met someone genuine but put bits and
pieces of others who hurt me onto them
and declared them the fakest thing known to man
An there has to be a reason why I scare people away
And the ones who care enough to tear down these

intentionally built walls
when they get to the inside they are still stalled
Stalled by this mind that continues to work overtime
And convince me that everyone around me is telling lies
But still there has to be something more for me
Something more beyond these grimy streets
Something more in between my nervous heart beats that pound and pound against
my chest like heavy anvils that equivalent to the thoughts that are constantly weighing on my brain
Over the years I've heard people tell me there is nothing wrong with me I just care about too much
So I tried to smoke weed but it only left me with more rapid heartbeats and extended and intense episodes of paranoia
creating another jail within my minds holding cell only silencing my yells
someone please tell me when will I be able to greet that something more
whether it's a person or a place anything's better than this place
where my mind is constantly moving at a fast pace
doing things like questioning the need for questioning
or wondering how many licks does it really take to get to the center of tootsie pop
but still there has to be something more for me
something more beyond these grimy streets
something more in between my nervous heart beats that pound and pound against my chest like
heavy anvils that are equivalent to the thoughts that are

constantly weighing on my brain
so what may seem to you as futile thoughts are not
thought out of vain
they are not just worthless chains of thought
they could potentially get me to that something more

Natural

Making the decision to be me in my natural state
Was a carefully thought out one
Finally deciding to stop running from who I am on the inside
And reflect it on the outside brought tears to my eyes
But most definitely not tears of sorrow but tears of joy
And you can't quite figure out why I chopped off years of relaxed drama
Aiming for perfection
And wore proudly my cut like a boy
And you can't quite figure out why this is important to me
Nappy hair don't make you a slave
Cause I am most certainly free
I am completely comfortable with my coarse curls
That is why I am different than most girls
This hair that is not worn by many women on TV.
Does not bring any insecurities to me
This is the way God intended me to be
And I'll no longer damage his image chemically
So keep your T.C.B.'s and Just 4 Me away from me
Because me making the decision to be me in my natural state
Was a carefully thought out one
Natural is how I came and it is how I'll leave
So I could care less when you point and tease

Because when I look in the mirror I see
A kinky, cool, coarse tumbleweed, caramel complexioned queen
So when you tell me I look pretty relaxed
I say thanks but I am beautiful
I'd rather have tight curls than that
My hair is the perfect reflection of me though my roots aren't long
They are surely strong
And sometimes I frown at the transitions I made
And reminisce about that girl with virgin hair and pomade
And though she broke combs she always dreamed of breaking records
That all vanished away when notions of straight haired perfection met her
After more time and reapplying the lye
I decided to stop running from who I am inside
And reflect it on the outside
Making the decision to be me in my natural state
was a carefully thought out one
I am embracing where I came from
Now wait and see what I'll become

Y'all Don't Know

Y'all don't even know how deep she can go
You'll don't even know how mean is her flow
You'll don't even know how bright she glows
You'll don't even know
But who fault is that? Surely, it's hers.
It's up to her to put in work and deliver her word.
She was curbed, call her scared or perturbed.
She took the wrong critics opinion into consideration regarding her work.
Being more than her work, but her worth she felt like she'd just been badly burned.
Robbed of everything she earned. But she let him take it, with her gift she could not make it.
She tried to revive it but, in this game, you cannot fake it.
But he had no God he was truly forsaken.
And although she's at rest everything you are speaking, she spoke it.
And when you can't find what to say you pick up your gun and tote it.
Whether literally or figuratively you fired your weapon with the intentions to kill, steal, and destroy.
And now that I see you had it out for me regardless of the fact that you're thirty and I'm seventeen you envied something inside of me and made it your duty to make it subside in me.

My guard was down I didn't know better I was ignorant to the fact that you are scum and I'm better!
Bet her, bet him I bet they'll all have smiles on their faces when they reminisce over when I gave them hope, I told them they could win, if they just trusted that light within.
I stumbled off the path of righteousness and I learned a lot and I found it again, because after all I do have faith in that light within.
Call it God, call it Allah, call it Shiva, call it Yahweh, call it Elohim, call it me, call it the Supreme but just know that you could never ever do it again.

"Friend" or "Foe"

I can see your dishonesty from a mile away.
I can smell your fraudulence on any day.
I can sense your low self-esteem, but others are naive because their intuition isn't as keen.
You have issues & don't get me wrong we all do but yours can potentially drive you downhill & you're dying for me to be a passenger, but I've concluded that's a bumpy ride.
You will never understand me because you haven't even mastered yourself, you lack goals, responsibility, & you constantly endanger your health.
It's funny how first impressions can change & someone so familiar can suddenly look so strange.

Codependent Connections

Reaching out to grasp my sanity through a cloud of
insane thoughts
and lessons that were taught
receiving failing grades
picking up the pieces and starting once again
I guess you can say I have tough skin
and a bleeding heart within
reading into your interior
your exterior's paper thin
wondering do we have what it takes to win
remember when you use to go out on a limb?
now I yearn for your attention again and again
day after day
you play this silly game
competing with the world
trying to earn yourself a name
you swear I do but on you I never place the blame
for time spent and countless words unsaid

you're my feet and without you through this water it's hard to tread
this is the feeling that I dread
I guess I'm getting a little ahead of myself
But I still pray to God you're in Good health
I love you but honestly not more than life itself
That's why I refuse to be a prisoner of thoughts of you
daydreaming about dreams coming true
days without you feeling blue
I fathom me and you being stuck like glue
and I have faith that one day my dream will come true
holding hands and skipping to our loo
god damn I'm a fool
kind of like I'm in love with a ghoul
with the power to scare my insecurities right the hell away
on any day
when going through a poetic drought I find inspiration in you

The Saga Ends

I don't know what to say any more than I know what to do
 and believe me I have the slightest clue of what's gotten into you
 or even what's gotten out of me concerning what we shared and how we used to be.
 things seem a little too still
 because I'd rather rocky cause at least then
I'd know we still have something going on
 now I have no idea what to call it.
I guess we're just friends with no ends
 no warm embrace for my arms to extend out to
 no kisses to intercept
just purples and blues where pinks and reds use to be
 yellow suns and love reruns
 now our program is cut off the air
nonexistent after only running for a short period of time
 I feel our love is spent but I still feel that we're meant

heaven sent you are but hell bound our relationship is
cause you can't seem to rock with me like you once longed to
I've summed it up to you feeling yourself nowadays
and me not having the freedom I once had before
so all I see are closed doors and missed opportunities
to relive what we shared and what we used to be.
damn, what has gotten into me
I don't long again and again over men or play with boys like toys
I remember when you acted as the perfect gentlemen
now I just want to hear your voice
but not really because I long for your presence after I hear your voice
do I have any choice?
Will you be here so I can rejoice
or just keep yapping with the noise?

Daydreaming

There is this guy, reminiscent of a God. No wings in sight but I'm sure he can fly.

We live through a love that I just can't explain and not because it's strange (although it is) but because I can't find the words beautiful enough to explain this union.

Needing not one ounce of explaining or justification, I have faith that over time our love will be remaining.

Visions of taking flight and one by one renaming planets in a universe where only we exist.

If you don't get the gist don't be pissed because I believe that everyone deserves this!

This type of love, no, but a unique love of their own.

It feels better than home as a matter of fact it is, cause home is truly where the heart is and believe, NO, just know it's in you.

Along with undying admiration and faith beyond measure.

Through cycles of changing weather your heart warms

me like my favorite sweater.

I don't have to wish for you to stay eternally because love endures at all cost no matter the circumstances.

You inspire me and with each day that passes you desire me on a more intense level than you have already had me. Fresh, each day feeling like the best, anticipating the next, and your love has me vexed.

And even though I have the slightest idea of who you could be I am 1000% sure that this poem, one day will become reality.

Part-time Daddy Blues

I hate to keep making you the topic of my pieces.
But when my heart's broken therapy is in my writing it acts as glue to reattach the pieces.
I've experienced more heartbreak from you; one man.
When you're the only one who shouldn't cause me pain I'll never understand.
From a little kid who never attended a father daughter dance.
To a pre-teen who could say she never held your hand.
From an adolescent looking for love where it never even lived.
To a woman who resents you for the things you never said or did.
Some say it's pointless to be sad over you & countless times I have agreed.
But you can't ever really neglect a wound that never ceases to bleed.

The Realization

You can't have rain without sun rays

You can't have joy without some pain

You can't always suffer loses without some gain

Because in falling there's a lesson especially if you got up

& even if you stayed there you have knowledge of what tripped you up

See we live free, think in captivity, & are scared as hell to be

Brave enough to face the unseen but too coward like to truly believe

Full but still face greed

Starving & with great pride turn down a hand that isn't reluctant to feed

See, are we oblivious to our own insecurities or are we reminded of them every waking minute so we use them as a crutch & consider them something we need?

Taking journeys & getting more acquainted with me has always gotten me higher than any weed...

But I still use to roll a blunt when I felt like things were too much & stuff went sour & I caught the brunt

Sour times called for diesel highs

Countless laughs until we freed our minds

But when we come down we realize we only wasted time

Because after the haziness in your eyes & the therapeutic trips in your mind subsides

You come to terms with that fact that reality is still on time..

Currently in the present

Presented in your presence

Most will let these cycles prevent them from perfecting lessons

But if you don't learn from your shortcomings I will from yours & mine

Striving to be, do, & live better

I swear I have a mistake shrine

& don't get me wrong I appreciate it

Because if I've never gone through anything how could I ever truly say I made it.
So when life gives you tests remember it's up to you what you do because after all you grade it
Whether you pass or you fail always remember to save it
Each & every experience makes your life your own
& when you are content with it all in my opinion that's when you can say you've grown.

She

She is already occupying the space as someone else's want & need to write, but every time I pick up a pen or tap on a key I want to write about how I can clearly see her tap into me & vice versa. I pray that she is not fazed by cliché things like all queens deserve kings because something about her soul is synonymous to me. This queen probably feels she doesn't deserve a thing, maybe because she's been heart broken by many of whom were potential kings. Just when I felt there wasn't any capability of receiving & extending love inside of me I saw her eyes and I felt like there was hope...Eventually this queen will learn to love & whether it's a queen or a king I'll always remember it was a queen that subconsciously let me know I was capable of such a beautiful thing.

Pregnant State of Mind

Now I understand why those boxes I get out.
I've always been free I just haven't discovered my route.
Sometimes it's so easy to wallow & pout but in this very moment I have areas to scout
Areas of my life that tell my unique tale
And areas of my heart that are deeper than a well
Spirit so bright it could light up any sky
Soul so uplifting its better than any high.
I have to find my route, what I'll do in this world
Not what makes me money but what truly joys my world
I have to find my way It may be not so far
but I now understand that getting there helps you discover who you are.
I'm twenty & I'm growing every single day
Not perfect but trying not to let negativity get in my way
But with wisdom I have seen that a lil' dirt can help us grow
It's all about your courage & the seeds you choose to sow
I'm loving me the woman I am today, and I am hopeful that I'll continue to change for the better in every imaginable way
I'll keep myself inspired & look for all the Good
Keep my head up always after all I really should
I'm proud of me for all that I am
I can't worry about what I do & do not have

Because if it goes I have me & the strength in my stand
My stride, my confidence, & my art
No one can ever take the compassion of my heart
though sometimes it was hiding when I spent days in the dark
My spirit longing, thirsty, in need of a drink
I call it love & it's amazing because if the things it does
Allows me to forgive, admit, and apologize when I'm wrong
Allows me to look inside of me & compose the words to my life's song
Allows me to do good when there's a million reasons to do wrong
Allows me to stand up straight when it would understandable if I was not strong
To me love is like magic that never fades away
Puts a twinkle in my eyes at any given moment on any given day
We sometimes get so hurt that we wrap up in cocoons
But to be that beautiful butterfly you have you have to experience life and never forget love heals all wounds.

Staying True to Me

Raising this woman was no joke but a long road with twists and turns
Although I found countless laughs and smiles along my journey
I grew when I experienced hurt
Grateful to be, just here writing this piece
It's in these moments I lose all fear and my heart mind and spirit finds its peace
I light up in ciphers spreading knowledge and wisdom
No weed
But the glow is similar to a Christmas tree
I look back on that little girl Nowey, who I still am today just a little more wise with thighs, a true spirit and a conscious mind
Who doesn't concern herself with time but the sincerity of the rhymes
Raising this woman was no joke and a prize
Becoming a mother made me realize
The work you put in your words builds the foundation of your actions
The more time I spend writing poems that flow from my heart the less time I have for acting
I got that High definition vision but sometimes pictures fool you that's why I keep that closed caption

December...

Love from my daughter vital like that flowing water
Woke up with her smile on my mental kept me pushing and exposed mine like I'm receiving dental
I say Good Morning to the bus driver and thanks to the store clerks who assist me
How could you wake up next to sunshine in December and not be chipper?
Not be giddy?
I walk these cold streets praising God because her warmth stays with me.

I don't have one poetic thought flowing through my mind
And as you sit there and read these words I bet you can say that's a lie
Every feeling in my heart, every thought in my head, every word that flows from my lips
Never cease to live up to some truly poetic shit

I want to go to life, I want to go to love, I want to go to free
Completely comfortable being me
I want to go to the Sun and awaken Sons
Take a trip to the Moon and pass my hearts love down to my daughter sacred like a family heirloom
I want to go to beauty
I want to go to creativity

I want to go the destination that holds the most significance and divinity

You say where I want to go is always with me when I just be
Well what if I have the idea in mind but couldn't tell the place from my current space if it was right in front of me?
What if I have a place in mind but I spend so much time in one space that I altered the vision in my mind of where I should spend my time?
Then I get a picture
A beautiful image to see
My daughter
When I see her smile I realize it's not an image to see
It's a heartbeat to feel
Hands to hold
Stories to tell
Experiences to unfold
Minds to shape
Spirits to mold
Worth more than Gold

Merry Christmas

It's Christmas again & I'm spending it with you
The season to give & my wallet isn't filled with loot
It's quite alright because I have my Love & I'm extending it to an angel from the heavens above
My mother, my friend, and great support
To show you how grateful I am for you is a gift I could never afford
So I'll always write you poems that flow from my heart
And show my gratitude for you & your warm motherly heart
You do your job & you're actually the best
I can fly in my own thanks to you nurturing me in the nest
I can stand on my own thanks to you helping me through tests
I love you so much more than you will ever know
& this Christmas season I'll let my thanks show
You're always there for me reminiscent of a savior
So deep in my heart it's your presence I'll always favor
Cooking up them meals never holding the love & flavor
I'll frame these words of truth so you can finally have something to savor!

Progression

I was distracted, vision in fractions.
Moving back from the acting, the loose promises, and non-existent actions.
I'm tired of the boxes therefore I cannot go back in.
Looking back in time I was hurt but, in the end, I was refined.
I survived, I thought I was wasting time until I realized my story can become a rhyme that truly can transform lives.
Put an end to cries, replace hurt with hope. Open the doors to healthy mechanisms to cope.
More potent than dope, numbing empty lives & freezing time.
I used to appreciate being grounded until I discovered the climb.

Daddy's Off the Clock

I can't even publicly blast you
I'm busy looking past you
Gazing at my daughter doing more than the day before
She use to sleep 16 hours out of 24
Now she's on the move, ready to explore
Getting a little louder, growing a little longer
Inquisitive about her surroundings & gaining strength so she's stronger
She amazes me & has brought out things in me I've never seen
Your absence is not detected, she is happy & has no knowledge of being neglected
I will never speak bad about you to her because she will one day draw her own conclusions
Your love and care is simply an illusion
And I would rather you not be around at all than doing part time and subjecting her to confusion
You think you're hurting me by not supporting her but in reality you are the one that's losing.

Vampire

You want to use me. Abuse me & consume me.
Even with all proper tools, your work is of fools, please.
Run back to me when you are feeling so lonely. I don't want your fake love or your coldness to hold me.
There once was a time when I'd stoop to your level left my heart in pieces and my insides disheveled.
You will never grasp that power again; your miserable nature cannot corrupt my Zen.

Love's on the Run

I use to think I was too old to get butterflies.
When you're in love you say goodbye to if's, ands, buts, & whys. Time flies.
It's been a while since someone touched my heart & made an impact on my soul.
It's been a minute since my love truly had a home.
The frivolous conversations, silent lies, & sour times leave you in a jaded nature.
Lacking the patience to truly trust and keep waiting for that knight in shining armor that you substantially relate with.
We let the physical entrance us instead of pure love that enhances us.
We hold tight the idea of what looks right, when it's our kryptonite.
We put up with hella shit at night and by day better days are on the run, that's not love & it's certainly not fun.
See we got it confused, somewhere down the line some of us got things fused.
Love & relationships are on two different levels.
Love is what connects us relationships are labels so that people know we're together & we convince ourselves one day things will get better.

Purpose

It wasn't until I stopped talking, I could truly write.
Carrying my thoughts are heavy enough I can't juggle your life.
I try to articulate my hearts words.
I can't tell my story when being bombarded with your suggestive verbs.
I had to take a step back & reconnect with me.
Honesty is the fee & enlightenment is what I reap.
I have a baby girl now I'm taking mental notes.
It's only a matter of time before I'm tested, I can't be out here resting.
I must stay sharp for Nia, she's my purpose I was blessed with.
So many things I want to tell her, even more I want to show her.
I'll sacrifice relationships if it means being an extraordinary mother.
Don't be jealous or salty if I don't answer when you call me.
My only obligation is to be there for my offspring.
I know y'all saying damn Mommy must have a life too, but that's my choice there's only so much I can devote my time to.

My Love

I have been lied to by people who were seemingly honest.
Manipulated by those who appeared to be principled & of high morals.
I was told "I love you" by men who just wanted my mind, body, spirit...
Nothing wrong with want but they wanted to own me & use me...they could never get away with abusing so they'd rather the amusement & constant confusion
Just ruthless.
The crazy part is. I remain their world.
One truth they all told is I'm no ordinary girl.
Of course I've faced adversity and at times I didn't win.
But what sets me apart is my shining soul & big spirit within.
If they would have known what to do with the jewel they stumbled upon.
They would have seen my hearts eyes through their hearts eyes
& it would have truly humbled them.
But instead of doing the work and digging through the dirt that covers their true beauty
They try to impress me & hype up their world
Not knowing these things don't phase me I'm not really a material girl
Yeah I like nice things that's no doubt...

But sell my soul, open my legs, believe you're my savior?
No that's too far out.
While you're claiming you love me, you don't even feel you deserve me
you're too busy thinking up ways to make me submissive & preserve me.
I'm not here for show, though I'm a beautiful sight to see.
I think.
I feel.
I cry.
I laugh.
I live.
I love. I BE.
So if you're one of those people that feel you need to buy my love
Just remember there is no price on the seas or the fluffy clouds above.
Just like they have been here and will be for many, many more
My love is just the same it's more valuable than anything that can be found at any store.
It cannot be duplicated & it's not finite like this body.
My love will always be stored, adored, & around forever more
it's truly that type of matter that can never be destroyed.

Let Me Explain. Me.

I told myself the next time I wrote I would write a poem that tells my listener exactly what I feel
and I bet those who have heard countless pieces are saying..."doesn't she do that already?"
Well here goes nothing & everything
the road was slow and steady but now I am ready to say exactly what's on my heart
I once feared this start
Let me no longer stall
updating the status of my art
I am lost & found
I am free & bound
I am everything different and alike
I am hot and cold
I am timid and bold
Who you see depends on the time of day
I am funny yet serious
I am coherent yet delirious
Who I am is contingent upon the energy present
I am Noel Dior
A free thinking, over analytical, Queen
With the will to help others and the wisdom to know when to bow out
I am a giver, a taker
A mover, a shaker
I am so many things wrapped up in one within
I'm spiritual yet religious

It's hard to tell when I'm kidding
I am as crazy & sane as can be
I have highs, I have lows
I have given & taken blows
But I promise I would never raise a hand in anger
I never experience danger although I befriend complete strangers
My heart and soul finds the God spirit within them
I am Noel Dior I will say once more
I am everything different & alike
I have strength in my words
I have power & might
And the faith to say & believe everything will be ALRIGHT

My Soul Speaks
Getting back to the music or shall I say me?

After a year of silence, I want to write

Smooth like bass-lines and rapid like sun-kissed hands striking African drums

I want to move men like water with my natural given wisdom

I want to relate to my sister's souls and mend some

I want to win some although the best of us lose some

True lights take their endings and begin some

I want to be so inspired that I'll never get tired of free-styling poems in my mind and spend all night writing them down

So I can remember

And inspire the soul of another member of this Earth we seek to try to get our purpose within reach

Just call me a knowledge leech because off of it I feed

With my wisdom, understand that it's love that I breed

My soul speaks

A Letter to My Father

Dad, you have always encouraged me to write.
Encouraged me to read.
Encouraged me to question.
Encouraged me to be.
Growing up in a sea of brown babies lacking Daddy's I was perceived as one of them.
But I had a Dad who I viewed as the most important man in my life.
Your absence made me dislike you and love you even more.
I knew you. We laughed, we shared experiences, we cried, we loved.
Every summer I would wish for you to come around, I prayed on the stars above.
I had memories with you & grateful I remained.
I know some kids who never knew their Daddy's name. You may think I am not proud of you and the man you have become
You always say you got to protect your heart and I know exactly where you're coming from
I love you and I learned a lot from our time apart
It's amazing how some people can never leave your heart.

Still Here

It took my life to feel like hell for me to get to know Noel
Ears covered, lips bind, eyes blind
It took all of this to dig deep in my mind
It took being victimized and a part of a crime
To get to know me and no longer deny
Who I am, who I was, and who I hope to become
It took being crushed and having little freedom
To see my new found wisdom
I'm working on the overcome
It took more than to confront the one
That made me feel my life was done
It took more than me running away
And finally recognizing the day
It took more than feelings less than strong
And having rights come out of wrongs
It took more than days feeling like night
and thinking nothing's ever right
Darkness void, cold, and so black
my feelings hurt and weights on my back
it took more than tears to form a sea
To pry to find the deeper me
It took more than pride locked up and mashed
Thinking that the key was trashed
It took more than my heart being slashed,
Seeing my life clash, wishing the present was like the past, If I could buy it how much cash?

It took more than flames around my heart and quivering inside the dark
It took more than heart as hard as bark
And more than wounds leaving marks
It took more than death looking like art
And finally recognizing my part
It took more than my pillow saturated with tears
And running away from all my fears
And constantly changing my hair
To bring out someone who wasn't there
The one who isn't there now will never come back
But the one who is here now, strength she does not lack

My Children Wore My Tears Today

Today my children wore my tears
A set for him and a set for her
They weren't tears of sorrow, pain, or regret
They weren't filled with the weight of things I'd rather forget
They weren't to water my eyes from dry because I couldn't sleep last night
They weren't a salty residue from the choices I've made in life
They weren't tears of resentment and everything that it breeds
They weren't tears of disappointment over a lack of vital needs
So why did my beautiful children wear mommy's tears to school?
well, it started with me waking up and waking them up too
My daughter, who is ten raised out the bed
and commenced to start her day and do what mommy said
I gathered up their uniform shirts and went to iron their garments
I immediately thought of things of which I could complain that fill my day with much disdain

Instead, I thought of how my heart has not been hardened
How my faith has been strengthened
How my forgiveness has been lengthened
How I have been forgiven
How I easily forgive
How I am so deeply grateful to lead this life I live
Oh the tears started flowing while I ironed their little shirts
I think of how my tears were a symbol of works
Works being alive through faith I've nurtured since a child
I cried through grateful eyes and now a childlike smile
A smile that I have earned and never knew it was deserved
Until I realized that I'm a phoenix that has risen after being burned
I pressed each shirt like it was the only job I had
I thought to myself how many tears my mommy shed
On the clothes of 4 girls, she had raised all alone
I give thanks, I give praise
Hallelujah! Today is a new day
God did a new thing He turned my mother's tears of sorrow into my tears of joy and veneration
The transmutation is cause for holy celebration
I know all too well I wore my mother's tears
went out into the world cloaked in all her fears

As mean words and stares from peers hit like daggers
and pierced like spears
I once questioned my existence here
If it's in the water, it's for sure in the tears
After all those years I realized we have to alchemize our gears
We either switch them or we ditch them
When it comes to new ideas, be bold and you pitch them
My children wore my tears today
There's a prayer in each one
That will set the tone for their day
And let Gods will be done

Poetic Prayer

Dear God, I need your help always. I am realizing now more than ever that I cannot do anything outside your will and be at peace. I need your love and your guidance. I need your strength and your kindness. I need your vision through my blindness. I need your support when I am trying. Trying to walk on the path that you have laid for me. Straight and narrow. Your eye is forever on the sparrow. I need your love through my body like marrow. I am at your mercy and your grace endures forever. I am alive and well because you breathed life and purpose into me. I am of sound mind because you lend me your thoughts. I am righting my wrongs because you lend me your heart. I now know it was never something to hold temporarily because your love is everlasting. You have been my comforter, my friend, my teacher, my father, my mother, my heavenly director. I am in awe of you. I am so grateful for your hand in my life. In Jesus' mighty and unmatched name, I am saved from the grips of poetic pain. Amen.

www.ingramcontent.com/pod-product-compliance
Lightning Source LLC
LaVergne TN
LVHW051513070426
835507LV00022B/3083